OCT   2015

For Billy George

JANETTA OTTER-BARRY BOOKS

Text and illustrations copyright © Susan Steggall 2015

First published in the USA in 2015 by Frances Lincoln Children's Books,
an imprint of Quarto Inc.,
276 Fifth Avenue, Suite 206, New York, NY 10001
www.franceslincoln.com

ISBN 978-1-84780-742-7

Printed in Shenzhen, Guangdong, China

1 3 5 7 9 8 6 4 2

colors

Susan Steggall

Frances Lincoln
Children's Books